Soul Retrieval

Reclaiming Your Authentic Self

by

Timothy P. Faust

LICENSED CLINICAL THERAPIST

with Barbara A. Brown

WRITER

UPDATED FIRST EDITION

February, 2020

Soul Retrieval
Reclaiming Your Authentic Self

Updated First Edition
© 2020

Published by Timothy P. Faust

Book Design by Will Pipkin
Copy That, Ashland, WI

ISBN: 9798619092059

Timothy P. Faust MSW

Harbor North Counseling
POB 3
Washburn, WI 54891

harbornorth1945@gmail.com

Office (715) 373-0480

Cell (715) 209-1045

Barbara A. Brown

POB 868
Bayfield, WI 54814

Table of Contents

source unknown

Introduction

by Tim Faust

I worked on this book at a local coffee ship with Barbara A. Brown, a friend and journalist. We met every week for over three years creating a draft hundreds of pages long. During each session we chose an inspiring quote which I would interpret as it might apply to inmates. At the time, we had no idea the work it would take to compile a book that had the potential to help inmates reclaim their authentic selves. It is our wish, hope and prayer that this handbook for change is a godsend!

Several factors and life events played a role in writing this book. My initial professional job after graduating from college was a juvenile parole officer for the State of Florida. I was 24. My guiding inspiration was author and psychiatrist Dr. William Glasser. I was working with teenagers in St. Petersburg, Florida who lived in poverty with most of them involved with gang activity. Glasser's writing and my undergraduate professor Dr. Alexander Bassin suggested an approach of having all of them attend groups using Glasser's theory of Reality Therapy (a means of helping them come up with a plan to live life by staying out of trouble). My position as a parole officer was not long lived. I found myself wanting to go west and find an even better way to help those who had a lifestyle of lock-up.

In 1971 I was introduced to a psychiatrist by the name of Foster Cline. He became a lifelong friend who was full of truths and wisdom at a young age. He gave me the opportunity to develop a different method of working with troubled youth, parents, families and individuals. It was at this time of my life when I had begun evolving into the person I was meant to be. But, as you know, life is always something that happens to you when you're making other plans. I am now in my 70's. Looking back I have gone through a broken marriage, difficult bosses, no money, alcohol problems, dyslexia and depression.

I have taught, trained, lectured and facilitated workshops from Alaska to Africa. There have been many guides and teachers who have greatly influenced my direction and purpose in life from my high school football coach, co-workers, professionals and friends, to my college professors.

Some have come into my life who acted as surrogate parents. I thank them all.

How or why this book got written indirectly had to do with the death of my mother. She didn't find sobriety from her alcohol and nicotine adiction until she was 60 years old. She became very active in AA and was instrumental in starting several 12 Step meetings in Buffalo, New York. I was amazed at the change in her life and intrigued with the wisdom of the 12 Step Program.

Years later some friends and I brought Ernie Larson's *Guide for Living 12 Step Program* to Fort Collins, Colorado. I was the national co-chair for this program for approximately a year and a half. Ernie Larson said, "Too bad you have to become an alcoholic or drug addict to share the gifts of this powerful program." When I became the national chairperson I went to a 12-step meeting every day for roughly a year and a half.

I researched Alcoholics Anonymous' origins in Oxford, England. Its basic principles are:

- self-examination,
- sharing with another,
- restitution or amends,
- conscious contact with God, and
- service to others (without demand).

These principles, or life scripts, have guided me throughout my time on planet Earth.

So back to my mom… as a gift to her spirit (she died in 2002) I decided to set up a *Guide for Living* group at the Bayfield County Jail in Wisconsin. (My wife Heidi and had I moved to Bayfield in 1996.) I had been a member of the Bayfield County Criminal Justice Committee and they were trying to find another way of helping inmates. Being locked up without some form of rehabilitation wasn't working. They were returning to jail, time and time again.

Every week, for 65 minutes I guided them through the principles of *Larson's Guide for Living 12 Step Program.* My original one-year commitment is now over fifteen years.

The inmates have become my teachers. As it is often said, *it's in giving that we receive.*

1

I really don't have a problem when I don't drink or do drugs. Bad things don't happen to me.

Inmate, County Jail

One thing we need to learn to do is get honest with ourselves. The 12 Step Program has adopted the Shakespeare quote "This above all: To thine own self be true." Spirituality and honesty go hand in hand. There are four things we can do to begin the search for our authentic self:

Find a healthy support system – In your daily living choose to be with people, friends and family that encourage or create a healthy and positive life style.

Gratitude – To change your negative attitude begin with gratitude. Be thankful for all that comes into your life even for your incarceration. Being locked up could be the beginning of the end of an unhealthy lifestyle. Gratitude is the cornerstone to finding joy, peace, and happiness.

Focus your life on doing the highest good – Focusing on the highest good is another way to understand and honor your higher power. In all things, be and do your best. Alcohol, drug use, anger, greed and inappropriate sexual behavior are distractions and do not allow you to become the person you were meant to be.

Ask for help – Ask and pray for the desire to change your life. There are behaviors in your life which damage you. Part of you takes pleasure in these behaviors because it is what you know, even if it's not in your best interest. Good things will come when you get it right and get the help you need.

2

My friend, why are you getting so upset? Why don't you just Zen pass him?

Dr. Larry Denmark

About 30 years ago I was driving over a mountain pass in Colorado with a friend, Dr. Larry Denmark. The speed limit was 35 miles per hour on the narrow and impassable road.

The driver in front of me was going about 20 miles per hour. I was frustrated. When I finally had an opportunity to pass the car, the driver stepped on his accelerator and wouldn't let me go by. I had a few choice words but stayed calm. I soon had a second opportunity when the road was wider with no oncoming traffic. Again he sped up and wouldn't let me pass! This time I used words that can't be repeated with children present. On the third opportunity he again denied me. Road rage surfaced inside me.

Larry said, "Tim, why don't you just Zen pass him?" I said, "Do you think this car has rockets?" Larry responded, "Let me show you."

We traveled about one mile down the road and Larry said, "Pull over and get out of the car." There was a side turn-out with a mountain path; we were at 10,000 feet. Larry said, "Come with me." We walked down the path for about five to ten minutes.

Larry pointed out because I was consumed with anger I was missing the beauty of that spring day, the mountains, flowers, and blue sky. We hiked back to the car and started back on our journey. Larry said, "You just took a Zen pass. You will never see that driver again." He was right. I didn't see that driver or his car again.

I ask you now, are there people, places and things in your life that you need to Zen-pass?

Walk away from
people who put you down.

Walk away from
fights that will never be resolved.

Walk away from
trying to please people
who will never see your worth.

The more you
walk away from things
which poison your soul,
the healthier you will be.

3

I have learned after almost 20 years in the prison system that there is a time to shut up and there is a time to speak up.

39 year old prison inmate

When we see something wrong, it may be our nature to get involved. Some of us believe God Almighty wants us to do this. However, once we get involved, speak our mind and give our opinion, we open ourselves up to possible negative consequences. There are times when it is best to say nothing and in your heart of hearts, say a quiet prayer instead. The could be as simple as "Great Spirit, take this problem and send someone who can heal it and make it right."

Many of us arrogantly believe we have the right answers and our belief system is the best. At times we operate on a gut feeling; however, if you grew up in an extremely dysfunctional home, very often your gut feeling can be wrong. This is why a 12 step program is recommended. In the program it is suggested that you have a sponsor who can listen and provide clarity on many issues. On a final note, choose your battles wisely and remember the Serenity Prayer:

> *God grant me the serenity to accept the things I cannot change, the courage to change the things I can, and the wisdom to know the difference.*

4

*Do not think of yourself as a slave to circumstance.
Do not think of yourself as weak or inadequate,
poor or unloved. Do not give power to old habits
of thought by dwelling on them and acting as if they
were true. If you feel yourself swept away by self-pity
or self-condemnation, set your mind to evaluating
and understanding and appreciating yourself
instead.*

James Dillet Freeman

Do we really know who we are or do we have old habits or thoughts that are not true? Growing up in our families of origin, we may have learned untruths and behaviors that take us off course. What we think is an authentic lifestyle is anything but. We also surround ourselves with people who support this unhealthy lifestyle.

If you've been in jail more than once, it should have given you information that says something is wrong with your lifestyle – not the judge, not the public defender, not the district attorney. Oh, they too make mistakes, but you know in your heart of hearts how many times you've been graced. Your complaint might be, "I was barely over the limit for drunk driving. How dare you (police officer) arrest me – don't you know you have real criminals to catch?"

In reality, you've driven dozens, if not hundreds of times, under the influence. Consequently, you can play the game, you can dance the dance, you can fiddle the tune, but the end result turns out the same. It's time for you to give up your old habits and to question your thinking. Turn your mind and energy toward constructive tasks and new ways of living. Learn to appreciate yourself in a new way.

5

You must pay for everything in this world one way and another, there is nothing free except for the grace of God – you cannot earn that, or deserve it.

Charles Portis
author of **True Grit**

The soul's purpose is one of joy and serenity, not suffering. In Sarah Ban Breathnach's book, Simple Abundance, she says, "Someone who loves you unconditionally is at the helm." She goes on to say that you are sustained by love that protects you, but first you must ask. We need to ask for direction, help and guidance. Only then can the power be switched on. We must, "Ask… Ask… Ask… then give thanks – wait – and watch what comes into our lives." Below is a prayer asking our higher power for the gift of change:

Author of all things that watches over us, God of the sun, the moon, the sky, the trees, the rocks, the water, and all living things, grant to me what is good and stable in my life. I am sick and tired of my old habits and poor choices. I am not capable of change without your help. Please grace me with your power, wisdom and those you would send my way that will direct, encourage and teach me to not fear or resist a new start or new way of life. For without change there can be no true meaning to life.

T.P. Faust

It is not the
strongest species that survives,
nor the most intelligent species
that survives.

It is the one that is the
most adaptable to change.

– Charles Darwin –

6

*Spirit speaks to you constantly throughout the
day. Today, adjust your spiritual satellite, tune into
the higher harmonic frequency for help and move
towards your authentic wholeness.*

Sarah Ban Breathnach

In 2009 I was consulting for an orphanage in Monrovia, Liberia.
Upon my arrival, the director of the orphanage took me to an
outdoor restaurant at the beach. Some friends of the director joined
us at our table. Roger, a man in his fifties, was with his 27 year old
nephew. During our introductions and brief small talk, Roger said,

> *My nephew is very smart and was educated in the United States.
> He has his PhD in engineering. His only flaw is that he doesn't
> believe in God or a higher power.*

I was curious so asked for more information. Roger said,

> *I am a very rich man. I have dual citizenship as my dad was
> Lebanese and my mom Liberian. I have houses in the U.S.,
> Liberia and Belgium. Like my nephew, I didn't believe in
> God until I experienced this traumatic event. About 15 years
> ago, near the end of the civil war in Liberia, I was working my
> successful diamond mine with my brothers.*
>
> *At that time, I didn't look the way I do now – I had a full beard
> and had not bathed in two weeks. I was sitting outside against a
> wall resting with my rifle next to me. All of a sudden three trucks
> full of rebels came into the camp firing their rifles, screaming and
> yelling. I will never forget how frightening this was. The rebels
> rounded up my brothers and the workers but it seemed like I was
> invisible, as they didn't approach me.*
>
> *I watched as they unloaded a man from one of the trucks and
> put him in a wheelchair. I knew he was the leader because he
> was giving orders. I was scared and was sure that my brothers,*

the workers, and I would all be killed and the millions we made in diamonds would be lost.

I stayed against the wall and for some reason the rebels continued to not see me. I believed I was going to die feeling helpless and hopeless.

I came up with a plan to run off into the jungle and save my own life when suddenly I heard screams! I knew who it was. It was coming from a teenage girl who would visit from a nearby village. I was afraid she would be raped and killed, so I thought, I was already dead, maybe I could trade my life for hers.

I got up slowly, reached for my rifle and walked towards the man in the wheelchair. He did not see me coming. Again, it seemed like I was invisible!

I was about eight feet from the leader with my weapon pointed at him and said, "My name is Roger. I'm prepared to die today, are you? Tell them to set the girl free or you are a dead man."

He gave the command to let her go and I yelled at her to run as fast as she could, back to her village. I then said 'What is your name? What do you want from us? Do you want to kill us?'

He said "No. We've been out of food and water for days now. We don't want to kill you. We just want your food, water and ammunition."

I told the rebels where our supplies were but I kept my rifle pointed at the leader. At that moment I still believed that even though the rebels got what they came for, I would be a dead man. Despite this, I turned my back to the rebels and, walked slowly towards my brothers, knowing I would surely be shot in the back. There was no gun fire. The rebels picked up the leader, put him in the truck and drove off.

I should have been killed that day but somehow I was graced. For me, this was my first encounter with God. I don't go to church, but every day I give thanks. After this experience I found myself to be more loving, more generous, and more at peace with myself. I now know there is a God.

7

We should celebrate our independence every day.

Jefferson Wright

The Fourth of July is the day the United States celebrates its independence. It honors freedom from oppression, from not being allowed to practice personal values.

My mother had difficulty with her alcohol consumption and didn't find personal freedom from that addiction until she was 60 years old, when her sobriety started. She had some hidden wisdom and claimed her sobriety date (the day she stopped drinking) to be the Fourth of July. She said, "I will have a whole nation celebrating my independence." One year later, she did the same with her smoking. Her values, her view of the world and her life, all changed with her non-dependency on alcohol and nicotine. For her, gratitude was celebrated every day.

If we find ourselves caught up in addictions and poor choices, there are natural and imposed consequences which make it difficult to celebrate who we really are. So, be smart. Ask for help and become who you are meant to be and celebrate the real you every day.

We need to change.

If you go back to your same old ways, playthings, playmates, playgrounds, you will surely be back in the state's playpen.

8

Earth has no sorrow that heaven cannot heal.

Thomas Moore and
Susan Hayward

A Guide for an Advanced Soul

Our poor choices, misuse of drugs, alcohol, anger, sexual behavior and dishonesty has had a negative impact on our lives and those around us. The consequences have been a stream of lawyers, judges, jailers and a life of continual lock-up. How "unfun!"

What a waste of time! But when you ask for help from the Creator of the Universe, the God of your understanding, healing can take place. It's no accident you are where you are. It has been said, "If you continue to do what you've always done, you'll get what you've always gotten." We may think our behavior has been so terrible we cannot be forgiven, nor can we change. This is not true.

Even if you have taken another life and are truly remorseful, you can be forgiven at some level. Healing starts with a whole new way of looking at the world that includes rethinking values and rearranging priorities.

Making amends is a huge task – to the victim, the victim's family, to yourself, to your family, to your higher power. Amends can be direct or indirect, depending on the circumstances and seriousness of the misconduct. The world is drastically different now from the way you thought it was. For some of you, your new life must be a life of service; one of helping others with a spirit of gratitude and love (even if you must remain incarcerated).

This new path, with the passing of time, will take you to a place of peace of mind and serenity.

9

The most difficult thing in life is to know yourself.
Thales

Getting to know yourself is really a good thing. Who are you?

If you had to give six adjectives to describe yourself, three positives and three negatives, what would they be? Sometimes we are stopped or detained in our life and we enter into a place of limbo or time out called jail. This is not bad. You may think it is, but for those who want to change, it gives you the opportunity to think and self-examine.

Who am I? If I don't make the changes I need to make will I spend more time locked up, ruin all of my relationships and move towards self destruction, poor health or death?

For those of you who have been using meth, how are your teeth? For those of you using alcohol, how is your liver? For those of you using dirty needles, do you have hepatitis or another chronic disease? Is it time for a change? Is it time to become the person you are meant to be?

William James once said, "If you want a virtue, act as if." In other words, fake it until you make it, or pretend and act as a loving person and soon the rewards will be so great you won't go back to what you were.

Our time on planet earth is limited. If you decide to take that first step there are others who have been where you are and they will gladly give of their time to help you become the person you always wanted to be. The questions become, "Do I like who I am? Am I willing to take risks to become the person I was meant to be?"

10

Many people die with their music still in them. Why is this so? Too often it is because they are always getting ready to live. Before they know it, time runs out.

Oliver Wendell Holmes

Sitting in jail or prison is hard. We may become numb and don't feel anything.

Being locked away puts us in a deep freeze where time stops. Hours turn into days; days turn into weeks, months or years. We try and take one day at a time, not looking too far into the future because it just frustrates us and makes us sick and angry. We think about our children, our spouse, our brothers or sisters, mom and dad and we make mental notes about how we want to be when we get out. We say, "I won't drink anymore. I won't steal. I won't cheat on my spouse. I will spend time with my children."

We have good intentions but often what happens after our release is only short-lived. It may last for a week or a month and then we get back into the rhythm we have always known. It is that old familiar tune – it is our comfort zone and we can't or we don't want to give it up. We return to old habits. But if we stay away from the people that encourage us to make poor choices life can be different.

Our relationships can improve and we can become a responsible provider in a way that allows us happiness, joy, and love. It is time now to live. It is time to play your music. It is time to come alive before your time runs out.

11

*One of the greatest gifts of the mind is in learning
how to tolerate people and problems in our lives.*

Helen Keller

Most of us don't do well tolerating people who have beliefs different from ours or putting up with other people's negative behaviors. It is difficult when someone doesn't think what we're thinking, do what we do, or believe what we believe. This is an important lesson that must be learned.

We all have a breaking point, but when you are incarcerated you learn quickly that your anger won't be tolerated by a jailer or the jail system. One of the greatest gifts we've all be given is the freedom of choice: *When do we speak up and when do we say nothing?*

You don't have to confront everything. Pick your battles wisely! There are many lessons to be learned when living on planet earth. If you don't get it the first time you are locked up, don't worry, there are thousands of jails in this country and the captain of the jail will leave the nightlight on and provide you with a cot, hot meal and a change of wardrobe.

12

I am a thinking, feeling, breathing human being just like anyone else except for the disease inside of me – alcohol and drug abuse. But I am a talented person in spite of my problems and I have a lot to offer.

24 year old county jail inmate

Are you sad about the way your life has gone?   Are you unhappy because your children or significant other is not in your life?   Have you lost your job or can't find work?   Do you feel rejected or abandoned?   Do you think you failed with your family?   Do you have feelings of powerlessness?   Do you search in your mind for answers and don't know what to do?

These are all good questions you may have asked yourself; being locked up certainly provides plenty of time to think. Have you created a plan as to how your life will be different when you get out of jail?   If your plan doesn't include recovery and sobriety your life will not change. By going down the same old road of old friends and old hangouts, you're destined for a life of misery. Your talents and gifts will be buried or cease to exist.

A young man serving time in lock-up said it best,

*You need to change the Three Ps – if you go back to your same **Playthings, Playmates and Playgrounds** you will surely be back in the state's playpen.*

Do not ever, ever, ever give up!

You have value,

you have gifts,

and you have a place
in the universe.

13

*Everyone who got where he is
has had to begin where he was.*

Robert Louis Stevenson

Many cultures of the world talk about circles, which have to do with beginnings and endings. When you look at a full circle, where does it begin and where does it end?

It has been said that God, the Creator, Great Spirit, has no beginning and has no end (the Alpha and the Omega). In the circle of life we have a beginning and an end to our life on planet earth. If your beginning has gone foul, it's never too late to start over and begin where you are right now. If you are serving time you have probably gone to jail or prison more than once and if you keep coming back, you are traveling in a circle.

Have you ever watched a dog chase its tail? If the dog does it too long you say the dog is crazy or loco. Isn't it insane for you to keep coming back through the "revolving door", back to the gray walls, brick and mortar of the prison? Have you not hit your bottom? Is this a lifestyle that you will never change?

It is time for a new beginning, regardless of your past. It is time to live a life that doesn't include incarceration and wearing the uniform of the jail or prison. This can be done, metaphorically speaking, by wearing a different spiritual garment. It begins with honesty – with yourself and with others. It begins where you are right now. We are mostly a result of the decisions we make – and also the decisions we don't make.

14

The gem cannot be polished without friction, nor man perfected without trials.

Chinese Proverb

When we've hit our bottom and we are in great despair, new doors open and new teachers appear. We begin to realize that maybe our choices have been damn poor. We're all diamonds in the rough, which means we're all capable of changing and becoming a valuable person in our society.

This is not easy. We must be open to change and ask our higher power, our Creator of the universe, to come into our lives and only then can change take place. Some of us say, "I don't trust a higher power and I need to do it myself." That type of thinking never works because when we have become our own higher power, we do not see what I call "true north". This thinking detours us off the road of recovery and keeps us living in a false reality.

Self-examination and the sharing of our character defects are critical. It is also paramount that we make amends for the wrongs we have done. Belief in a higher power is not optional and helping another is essential. Having a higher power doesn't mean some authority has dominance over you. Just for today, allow friction by opening yourself to a new way of thinking and begin to become the person (gem) you were meant to be.

15

I am not interested in the pursuit of happiness...
I am interested in pursuing a truth, and the truth
often seems to be not happiness but its opposite.

Jamaica Kincaid

Going to the truth can be difficult. At first it can leave you helpless and hopeless. M. Scott Peck, author of *The Road Less Traveled*, said, "The truth will set you free – but first it will make you damn mad."

Being locked up can allow you to self-examine your life and without self-examination, life has no boundaries. When you live each day being honest with yourself and with those around you, good things begin to happen. It may not promote happiness at first but it will change your life. It will keep you from wearing the uniform of the day for the jail or prison and upon release those around you will begin to trust you.

Trust is a basic building block to relationships. The old you that used to pursue happiness by manipulation, stealing and lying will cease to exist. For many a dishonest lifestyle was learned during childhood. When you wanted something you cleverly conned and took what you wanted from a friend or foe. Often drugs and alcohol played a large part in how you behaved and have led you down a dark road, and if not challenged, you will end up with loss of life, limb or permanent lock-up.

16

Successful people keep moving.
They make mistakes but they never quit.

Conrad Hilton

We all make mistakes. Some of our mistakes have greater impact than others.

Some of our mistakes are small and we can brush them off and say, "No big deal." Other mistakes will stay with us for a lifetime, such as drunk driving and taking another person's life. This is where the spiritual component becomes important.

When you make a mistake that is so big it darkens your soul, you want to give up. If you give up and don't walk the path to make amends for your mistakes, then life as you know it will not change. A more powerful and life giving choice is to keep moving.

Always reach for a better life away from violence, dishonesty, drugs and alcohol. The bigger the mistake, the more you have to ask for help and direction from others around you, and especially your higher power.

For some of us our mistakes are so great our life no longer belongs to us – it becomes a life of service to others. One can find peace and serenity by finding purpose in helping others. Don't quit. Keep moving towards the goodness of your life and doing your highest good.

17

*I didn't have any self-love. I hated myself with a
passion. I thought I was unlovable but in recovery I
learned it was the drugs and alcohol in my body that
I hated and not the real person inside.*

Inmate, county jail

For many of us at some point in our life we learned not to have
feelings. We have frozen our emotions of love, guilt, anger, fear,
worry and sadness. On the surface we pretend to be okay but deep
down inside we know what we are doing won't bring us serenity or
happiness. We know our values have been compromised. We are a
person we don't like anymore and the truth is, we want to become
the person we were meant to be. We want to change and we know
we can change. We are teachable if we can let go of our denial and
stinkin' thinkin'.

Up to this time our choices have been poor and have left us
powerless. Our family, work, health and our authentic self, have been
put aside. It is only when we get the toxic chemicals out of our body
and find sobriety that we can become lovable. Let's hate the toxic
distractions and not our true self. There's who you genuinely are,
and then there's who you think you are. The former is a truth, the
latter is an untruth.

An excellent way
to go through the day
is to think kindness.

If you have low self-esteem
and don't really like who you are,
I suggest trying one
random act of kindness a day.

18

Nothing changes until you do.

Unknown

I once asked my Higher Power, "Will you help me?" Nobody came. It was then that I realized that my Higher Power was within me and healing begins with me.

In Sarah Ban Breathnach's book, *Simple Abundance*, she writes about "answered prayers." She states that very often we have not been praying for the right thing or in the right way. She goes on to say, "We may pray to meet our soul mate, instead of praying for the grace to become the (person) our soul mate would be attracted to... or we pray for a certain outcome in any given situation, when what we should be praying for is peace of mind, no matter which outcome occurs."

Change is all about the right attitude. Don't underestimate the Great Spirit, the Creator, Christ, or the God of your understanding. Our need is known before we ask but we must ask from our heart.

Be open to all that comes into your life and always know that in most cases we are the ones who need changing in order for our spirit to soar.

19

Vision is perhaps our greatest strength. It makes us peer into the future and then shape the unknown.

Li Ka Shing

How we view the world is critically important. Ernie Larson said it best, "What we live with, we learn. What we learn, we practice. What we practice, we become. And what we become has consequences."

Yesterday, I was driving to work with a broken windshield wiper on the driver's side. It was snowing, wet and cold. When I started driving my vision was clear, but then I got behind a truck throwing ice, dirt and sleet onto the windshield. My vision instantly became blurred and I could not see.

Even though the road conditions were dangerous, I felt I needed to get around the truck and waited for an opportunity to pass. But my vision of oncoming traffic was not clear. I passed anyway. By the time I got around the truck my windshield was a mess and I could hardly see. My decision then was to pull my car over to the side of the road and clear my windshield. I could see again. I felt safer. As soon as I saw a service station, I pulled over and replaced the damaged wiper.

Our life can be very much like this story. Maybe it's time for you to pull over and replace your windshield wipers and get a better vision.

20

*Do not go where the path may lead. Go instead
where there is no path and leave a trail.*

Ralph Waldo Emerson

Psychologists say if you had a good first three years of life with a
healthy upbringing, your mom and dad didn't smoke, do drugs or
drink during pregnancy, and were pretty healthy people, chances are
that your life is going to go pretty darn good. But what if your mom
was a drug addict and your dad was in and out of prison, or you
were shuffled around from house to house in the early years of your
life? The odds are pretty high that you will be locked up, for what
you lived with you learned and practiced and those behaviors can
bring negative consequences.

The question is, can you make changes? Can you be happy?
Can you stay off probation, parole, or out of the judge's courtroom?
I don't know if you can, but I do know that there is a loving, caring
God that wants great things for you. And should you choose to take
a path that is different than that of your parents, it starts with getting
all the help you can get.

It won't be easy. Your gut feelings will tell you to go the other
way. Taking one day, one step at a time, could make a difference.
You must realize that you do have a choice. Find humility, ask for
guidance and get out of your own way. Pray and surround yourself
with good people. Stay away from drugs and alcohol, and discover
the importance of a good night's sleep.

21

There is more hunger for love and appreciation in this world than for bread.

Mother Theresa

Our parents can provide house or home for us. They can feed us and provide the fuel for the furnace that heats or cools the house. They can give us a bed and a roof that doesn't leak but what we truly long for is love and acceptance. We can persevere with love, acceptance and care.

This is the magic that makes us human. It is what makes or breaks a relationship. It is what brings respect from people around you and others in the community. When you have support and love you try harder. But if love and appreciation are missing in your life, then you probably don't trust people and this makes it difficult to accept direction, help, support and love.

You have learned to go about life on your own with an "attitude" which can return you, again and again, to a life of poor choices, lock-up, or mental illness.

22

Our purpose in life can be clouded by an unidentified learning disability.

T.P. Faust

If we do not have an authentic purpose in our lives – something that is meaningful, a direction, and an excitement about life – we get distracted. We drift, get easily bored and make poor choices. I believe we are all born into this world with gifts, and our gifts appear through finding purpose. Gifts do not all appear at once; it seems like they are on an individual timeline.

When I was young I stuttered. It was shameful and embarrassing for me. My reading skills were poor. I had dyslexia, but no one knew about this learning disability at the time I was growing up. I felt lazy, crazy and stupid and I pretty much failed everything in high school. To stay with my class I went to summer school each year and was able to graduate high school. Albeit at the bottom of my class. After serving active duty in the U.S. Marine Corp, I went to a community college where my learning disorder was identified.

At that point my life changed. My gifts began to emerge. I gained self-confidence. My stuttering stopped. I eventually became a good public speaker – I could talk to groups of 50 – 200 people with energy, pizzazz and enthusiasm – without stuttering! I eventually went on to graduate school where I graduated with high honors – definitely no longer at the bottom of my class!

Could there be a block that is clouding your purpose? Attention deficit disorder or another learning challenge? Depression? Anger? An addiction to drugs or alcohol? Ask for help.

Take a risk for success in discovering your purpose by working through the baggage of the past and becoming a gift to yourself, family, friends and the world around you.

He who focuses exclusively
on his own needs often
doesn't end up with very much.

We need to learn
how to be giving of our
TIME – TALENT – TREASURES.

23

Never be afraid to tread the path alone. Know which is your path and follow it wherever it may lead you. Do not feel you have to follow in somebody else's footsteps.

Eileen Caddy
Footprints on the Path

When we have felt loneliness, pain, anger, resentment, rejection, abandonment or betrayal it hurts. We may feel all alone and we go to what I call the "cupboard of relief."

In the cupboard of relief you may choose to use drugs, food, sex or anger to relieve your pain. It gives us temporary relief but if our pain resurfaces by the same or another event, we go back to what worked for us, even if it's unhealthy. Behavior repeated over and over becomes habitual and eventually steals our spirit – our soul becomes lost to the power of addiction. Over time we begin to believe that this is who we really are or think this is our authentic self. It's not. It's a false reality.

Change is optional for us. It means taking a different direction down a different road. This type of change is called many things in many languages, but to simplify, it is the "road to recovery." Be careful not to follow in the footsteps of a family member or a friend that will lead you to a dead end. There are many paths to walk, choose wisely.

See the *Living Your Authentic Life* map on page 112, Appendix D.

24

I've been locked up for 39 days and my own energy (life force) is coming back. I've been dependent all these years on pills that gave me energy from the outside.

29 year old inmate

In recovery, to keep us from going back to jail or prison, we need to look at where and how we attained our energy. Are we dependent or co-dependent on a person, a drug, or illegal, manipulative behavior? The list goes on and on...

It's said, *We are what we eat.* I say, *We become how we live our daily lives.* As mentioned previously in this book, Ernie Larson said it best,

What we live with, we learn. What we learn, we practice. What we practice, we become. And what we become has consequences.

What are your dependencies? Do you keep going back to the same man or woman who physically or emotionally abused you? How much money would you have in the bank if your addictive and co-addictive behavior would come to an end?

Some have a nicotine habit which costs them thousands of dollars a year. The list of addictions is endless, as is the cost of maintaining them. Think of all the nice things you could have or vacations you could take, or time you could spend with your children. How might life be different once you begin the journey of change? Only you can get yourself off the merry-go-round; change comes from within.

The bottom line is how we love ourselves and love others. Sometimes God's blessings or miracles come disguised, like being locked up and not taking the drug of your choice for 39 days. Allow yourself to accept the blessing.

25

The most beautiful things are not associated with money; they are memories and moments. If you don't celebrate those, they can pass you by.

Alek Wek

I have early memories of my son and attempting to teach him about the God of the Universe. Living on Lake Superior, I owned a 24 foot sailboat aptly named Sea Otter. On Sunday mornings we would often motor over to Madeline Island, tie up the boat at the Beach Club restaurant, and walk to a nearby church.

One Sunday morning my friend and colleague Dr. Dale Irwin joined us for the excursion. After docking, we went to the church to attend Sunday services. My son was 12 years old at the time and was not very interested in participating in church-related activities. He usually had a pencil and paper and drew pictures during the service. Being the father that I was, I did not force the issue.

After church we returned to the Beach Club, played some pool, ate our lunch, and returned to the sailboat for our $2\frac{1}{2}$ mile sail back to the mainland. The sails were set and off we went. The wind was about five to six knots and we moved along but not at a racing speed. My friend Dale was seated in the back of the boat enjoying the sun, blue sky, water and the sail.

Out of the blue my son said, "I can swim faster than we are sailing." My response was, "I don't think so." In the next moment my son suddenly took five racing steps and flew over the top of the head of Dale straight into the water, like Johnny Weissmuller out of an old Tarzan movie. My son started to swim. Yes, he was a good swimmer; yet the boat quickly left him in its wake. We came about with the boat, put out the ladder, and my son climbed aboard. His spur-of-the-moment behavior left us amazed, astonished, and in awe.

This Sunday church adventure was an attempt to teach my son about the Creator, but instead we learned the value of our relationships and created an amusing memory we did not want to lose. For us this time was really a time to bond and I have learned in my older years how important it was and is to spend time with the people we love.

The truth is that the God of the Universe can be found in all of life, not only in a church. It can be found on the water, in a pool hall, on a ski slope, sharing a meal, on a mountaintop, on a hiking trail, in a jail cell or in a hospital room.

> *Thank you, son, for our special times together. In our spirits and in our time together God exists. Please pass these lessons learned to your children and to their children.*

As I have said before, there are always three or more ways of doing anything, including how we understand or believe in a higher power. It is true that in most cases it is never too late to establish healthy memories with our spouse, family, children and friends. We can erase the bad memories by establishing healthy good memories.

Even an airplane needs a lot of runway behind it to take off. Build a runway of memories with the people you love.

26

Learn to be silent.

Pythagoras

One way we can improve upon who we are is to shut up, shut up, shut up! Nobody likes to be told what to do and nobody likes to be told to shut up. However, we know that our words and manipulation of the past have gotten us into trouble and after a while we begin to believe our own manipulation or lies.

There's a time to speak up but more importantly there's a time to listen; there are times when silence is wisdom. Silence teaches us to be wise and to listen with both our ears and eyes.

Listening is a learned skill. When you listen, you gather information and process that information in a sober way and then share your views if the other person is willing to listen. Too many of us can't wait to talk and miss out on being a good information gatherer or listener. When we speak, we do not learn. When we are silent, learning is possible.

Try this: count to ten before you say anything and then count to 100 and say nothing.

What we live with, we learn.
What we learn, we practice.
What we practice, we become.
What we become, has consequences.

– Ernie Larson –

27

You must give yourself to love if love is what you're after. Open up your heart to the tears and laughter, and give yourself to love, give yourself to love.

Kate Wolf
musician and songwriter

Songwriter and artist Kate Wolf died too young. She died in December 1986 when she was 44 years old. The music that she gave to the world was full of love and inspired all who listened to it.

Kate Wolf said,

I live for the sense of purposefulness in the world; I could stop my life at any point and feel that my life has been worthwhile... I try to be as alive as possible and feel free to make my mistakes and try to be as honest as I can be with myself when I make a mistake.

The problem for many of us has to do with how we find love and purpose in our life so should we die tomorrow we know that we have made a difference on old planet earth. For many of us, being denied love as a child, we search and look for something or someone to love us. We focus our energies on being loved, rather than giving love. We open ourselves up to being loved by alcohol, food, marijuana, nicotine, gambling, pills and misuse of our sexual energy.

It is not love but rather poor choices that lock us into errors of thinking and addictive behaviors. If you want love, you need to give love to all the human beings and creatures around you and as Kate Wolf says, "It will be your greatest teacher and the best friend you have ever made."

28

The ascent of Everest was not the work of one day nor even of those few unforgettable weeks in which we climbed. It is in fact, a tale of sustained and tenacious endeavor by many over a long period of time.

Sir John Hunt

Have you ever heard the saying that life is not fair? I remember my mother telling me this when I was in the eighth grade.

There was a young man sitting next to me cheating on a test – he had a little crib note. When the test came back I had failed and he got 100 points. He had the audacity to boast about how smart he was! It made me angry.

I told this to my mother and she said, "It will come around. You may not see it now but your sincere effort will pay off in the future."

There are times when we don't do well in life and other times when we shine. What is always helpful to me is to remember to put forth my best effort. If at first you don't succeed, welcome to the club!

When you're locked up, you have one thing that you can use to your advantage and that is time. Use this time to make the changes and alterations necessary for a better life. In the end you will achieve a sense of well-being by staying with a program of honesty, healthy friends, abstaining from alcohol and drugs and finding an authentic purpose in your life.

Change takes time and failure can be another step toward success. Visualize the life you want, say it out loud, and them move to make it happen.

29

He who focuses exclusively on his own needs often doesn't end up with very much.

Anonymous

If we want good things to happen, we need to revisit what our kindergarten teacher taught us: To share.

We need to learn how to be giving of our **time**, **talent** and **treasure**. As a child, you may have learned to only take care of yourself because your parents weren't there for you. Or the opposite, your parents may have given you everything and you learned the word *entitlement*, which means "I deserve a good life and I really don't have to work for it."

I've seen this happen in cultures, religions, families and individuals. The attitude of entitlement steals who you were meant to be. The prophet that walked and preached two thousand years ago said it well, "It is in giving that we receive."

Try it, start small and see what happens. Unexpected happiness may appear when you help others. Good luck, be happy and remember that you are not the only one on planet earth.

30

*Imagination is everything. It is the preview of life's
coming attractions.*

A good place to start over in your life is to imagine what your life
might look like from this day forward.

Sometimes we believe that things are so bad in our life we can't
imagine changing who we are. If you go to an AA or NA meeting
and like what someone is saying, or see how that person acts, and
you imagine that you would like to be like them. It can happen. Be
open.

A step in this direction is to, "Act as if." Repeating a new behavior
over and over will lock in the change. Our blessings begin with us
and new visions in our imaginations. Never give up – it's never too
late to change.

Albert Einstein was not far off the mark when he said,

*Imagination is more important than knowledge.
For knowledge is limited to all we now know and
understand, while imagination embraces the
entire world, and all there ever will be to know and
understand.*

41

31

*When you compress charcoal it becomes a diamond.
When you are under pressure, if you are willing to
allow the darkness, pain and difficulties to teach you,
then you too can produce great gifts.*

Dr. Bernie Siegel

Nobody, I repeat nobody, likes pain, darkness, grief or depression.
We all want to feel good inside.

For many of us, we've had our share of rejection, abandonment
and betrayal. Should we do a timeline of our grief, we would be
amazed that we're still here breathing, eating and alive. It is out of
our difficulties where we learn from our hurts and mistakes.

We can use the past to help others and it is in helping others that
we help ourselves. However, if we choose poorly and find happiness
in a pill, a cigarette, a line up our nose, at the bar or in a bottle, it all
ends up making things worse.

We all have gifts and we all have talents but when we are distracted
by anger, sex, drugs and alcohol, we miss out on who we truly are.
What a terrible tragedy!

Remember that it's never too late to change, to become who you
want to be. Your piece of coal, if worked right, just might take the
shape of a precious diamond.

Be kind, be forgiving,
believe in yourself
and do not be afraid
to ask for help
for you are not alone.

Sobriety should be
our number one goal.

Surround yourself with people
who want you to have a good life.

32

*After serving six months of my two-year stay, I have
learned to listen to the jail breathing, how the doors
open, the jingling of the keys, the footsteps of the
jailers, the arguments of the inmates, the television,
the food coming, and every other noise.*

Inmate, county jail

Are you 18, 25, 32, 42, or 50 years old?   Are you male or female?
Did the cots in the jail hurt your back?   Are you tired of terrible
food?   Is your stay three months, six months, two or ten years?

After much time behind bars you too will hear the jail breathing.
It is something you swear to God that you will never return to. The
truth is, not until you're sick and tired of being sick and tired, can
things change. Some of us become comfortable and think we don't
need to change or can't change. Our early history has appeared to
have darkened our soul and we may feel helpless or hopeless.

The key to change has to do with helping another. That is why
sponsorship in a 12-Step program is so powerful. When you reach
out and help another you really help yourself.

An old friend had a philosophy that each day he would help
someone who needed help. This does not have to be done in a grand
way; it could be as simple as opening the door for someone. My
friend also knew that the power of giving and receiving were one and
the same.

For today, find someone you can help and practice my friend's
philosophy daily. It's true that in helping another or in asking for
help, you can keep from returning to the sounds of the jail breathing.

33

If at first you don't succeed, give up and go fishing.

Marvin Hecher

Sometimes we need a break in our life. We need to go to a healthy place where we can be restored. Respite and recreation can be very valuable.

For some, relief is found in their drug of choice; however, this will take you down a dark path toward death and destruction. Alcohol and drug addiction is a spiritual disease and a progressive disease. The disease makes promises of joy, love and adventure. Don't believe it. It's a lie and if it's not confronted it will steal the real you and convince you that the lie is the real you.

There are healthy things you can do to be restored. Talk with a friend, go for a walk, get into therapy, learn to ski, ride your bike, spend time in the garden, play with your cat or dog, or work on your car. Try painting, praying, meditating, taking a yoga class, or swimming laps. The list of restorative activities is endless.

Probably the most important things you should do today: eat right, connect with your higher power, sleep well, and exercise. When all else fails, go fishing.

34

*A day is never so bright as when
the sun is shining in the morning.*

Sir Walter Scott

Many of you who are behind mortar, brick and bars do not see the sun or the blue sky. How difficult. We know the sun, moon, stars, sky, rain, trees, grass and rocks are all part of our life. When honored, loved and appreciated the earth can heal the soul.

Psychologically, the sun has a great impact on our individual temperament. In the winter months, when it is dark and gray, we can feel low due to the reduction in sunlight, which triggers neurological and hormonal changes in the body. We call this *Seasonal Affective Disorder* (SAD). When we're not getting enough sunshine absorbed into the skin we produce insufficient amounts of Vitamin D. This affects the serotonin level in our body, the chemical in the brain that helps us to feel good and increases our energy. Dr. Daniel Skenderian, an expert in sleep disorders, notes that the lack of light and added darkness increases the production of melatonin, a chemical in the brain which contributes to low energy and sleepiness.

Whenever you get the chance to take a walk with nature and honor planet earth, be kind to her; she will be kind back to you. And don't forget that walking, running or any type of exercise in the outdoors can enhance your spirit and brighten your day.

Remember, upon your release, spend time in the outdoors and let Mother Earth begin to heal you. If you live in a climate with low sunlight in the winter months, consider an inexpensive supplement of Vitamin D3 that can be purchased over the counter in any pharmacy or grocery store.

35

*Relationships are more valuable
than material wealth.*

Ann Neivers

What are your values?

We must always examine our own belief systems. Do we put material things in front of relationships? Are we on our second, third or fourth relationship or marriage? It is true money and material things are important but relationships are more important.

Do you really know your child? Do you know their favorite color, their favorite food or television show, what they like to do most in the whole world? Have you gotten up with them in the middle of the night when they're sick and taken care of them? Do you spend optimum time with them – one-on-one, time just with them to have fun together and do something you both enjoy?

Our children need us. Our husbands and wives need us. Our families need us and we need them. It is difficult in this life to go it alone.

For the most part, the time spent locked up is wasted time, but it does get you to think. It's time that you make a change, become the husband, the wife, the mom or dad that your higher power wants you to become.

There will always be difficult times in your life, but during those times if we have a good solid relationship with a loved one, things just go better. Money and material things are necessary but get your priorities straight.

It's true: relationships *are* more valuable than material wealth.

36

There's no greater weakness than stubbornness.

Unknown

If your best friend or your mother or father had to give three adjectives (descriptive terms) to describe who you are, what would they say?   My intuitive hunch would be that one of these adjectives would be stubbornness.

My definition of stubbornness is doing it my way and not listening to what others have to say or going fast and unwilling to gather information or learn from another. Stubbornness is always built around mistrust. It feeds on self pride (ego) and fear. It is something that is learned early in your life, possibly through poor parenting or lack of parenting. Be careful not to blame by saying, "It's my parent's fault" and, "I am who I am." That kind of thinking, in my opinion, is another form of stubbornness.

You may think it's way too late to learn, but it is not. It is never too late to start over. Begin by having a willingness to understand that your opinion, your way, is not the only way. By having respect for another's opinion and truly listening, we can change.

Be strong. Give a little and understand *there are always three or more ways of doing any one thing*.

37

One act of random kindness at a time
will change the world.

Evan Almighty, the movie

When we wake up in the morning, it is the start of a new day. Sometimes our life has been so awful that the only thing we can do is take one day at a time.

An excellent way to go through the day is to think kindness. If you have low self-esteem and don't really like who you are, I suggest trying one random act of kindness a day. You don't have to do these random acts of kindness in a grand or big way. It could simply be letting someone in line ahead of you, or opening up the door for someone, or leaving a bigger tip at the restaurant. It could be saying a kind word or not saying anything when you want to say words of anger or meanness. The list is really endless.

This will change you and the world around you. The more random acts of kindness you do, the better you feel about yourself, and the world as you have known it will become a better place.

38

Enthusiasm is one of the most powerful energies of success. When you do a thing, do it with all your might.

Ralph Waldo Emerson

Success is not easy. Society judges us by our effort and our successes. While our efforts are paramount, we are not responsible for the outcome.

We must keep this in mind when working toward change. We need to put forth all of our effort but sometimes it is three steps forward and two steps back. We must never give up, for as you know, life is always something that happens to us when we're making other plans.

There are elements, people and events that happen to us with no foreseen predictability. Go easy on yourself. Stay with the program and remember a slogan from AA's Big Book, "Spiritual progress and not perfection." Sometimes success arrives instantly but frequently it arrives after a long passage of time.

Realize you are not in control of the universe. You are not the boss. You are not God. Whatever the circumstances, stay with your goal, put forth an honest effort with all your might and sweet success will come.

It has been said
addiction is a spiritual disease
and the beginning of recovery
is the admission that
we are powerless...

and that there is power
greater than ourselves...

and that we
turn it over and ask for help.

39

*When the spirit does not work with
the hands, there is no art.*

Leonardo da Vinci

Have you ever been in a bad mood, when nothing seems to go right and life just seems out of sorts?   My father-in-law has a word from his childhood, **benoud** that he learned from his Dutch grandparents. It means, "I'm not quite here and I'm a little melancholy."

It's certainly normal to have this feeling on occasion, providing it's temporary. However, if you're living this way all of the time, it's time to ask for help. Our spiritual being needs to be in harmony with our physical body. When it's not, we say and do things that can cause problems and we do not accomplish tasks in our work world and/or in our personal lives. Leonardo da Vinci, the artist that he was, was very aware of this concept.

We have three parts to our being. One is the **physical** being, the second is the **psychological** being and the third is the **spiritual** being. We do best in life when all three come together in harmony. After self-examination, working on ourselves is optional. We were never meant to live a life of sadness or depression.

Our higher power wants us to be happy but we have to make wise choices.

40

To dare is to lose one's footing momentarily.
To not dare is to lose one's self.

Soren Kierkegaard

Our life is full of daily problems, difficulties and even disasters. Sometimes we say to ourselves, "why bother?" and we slip into anger, frustration, depression and anxiety. We feel helpless or powerless, as if no one cares or gives a damn about our lives.

Believe it or not, this is not necessarily all bad. The famous Swiss psychiatrist, Dr. Carl Jung, might say to you if you were his patient, "Ah, this is good. Growth and change comes when we are truly powerless."

A friend of mine notes that this is a good example of a paradox: We become powerful when we admit where we are powerless. We move from a God-like attitude to a moment of truth when we ask for help from our Higher Power to guide and direct our life into one that is meaningful, loving and giving.

41

The world is too dangerous for anything but truth,
and too small for anything but love.

William Sloan Coffin

(as quoted every Sunday
by a local church pastor)

When we fall away from truth, we fall away from love. The problem for many is getting to honesty and love.

We create our own danger, misfortune, or disaster when we lie, cheat, manipulate and con. When we instead focus on the truth things change. Honesty and caring can create a world of love that attracts the right kind of people that affirm us and support us. It creates a new life that keeps us from restriction, isolation and incarceration.

None of us like to be locked up or "on paper" (probation). We hate to be controlled. It's time to replace your character defects with truth, kindness and love.

On the Road in Finding Your Authentic Self

• Eat Right

• Exercise Right

• Sleep Right

• Find Purpose

• Get Honest with
  Yourself and Others

• Help Others
  Without Demand

42

*Many situations can be clarified
by the passing of time.*

Theodore Isaac

When we're given bad news or we're in a crisis, our response could be anger, fear, shock, depression or denial. Our brain reacts with fight or flight behavior and many of us do what we've always done and it has gotten us into trouble. It's learned behavior and you know the rest of the story.

Some human behaviorists and existentialists suggest there are four ways that we can react to a crisis:

- do nothing,
- react with aggression,
- run away, or
- move to a higher process.

Of the four, the last should be the first, which means we must gather information and find another person to talk to about the problem.

Along with this higher process we need to turn over the crisis to our higher power. Then wait. This higher process keeps us from overreacting and it gives us time. Sometimes by just sleeping on the problem a new direction can be found.

It's true too that there are some situations where we are truly powerless and our worry is like a rocking chair – we go back and forth but go nowhere. It is time we find wisdom in our beliefs and dependency on a higher power as many situations can be clarified by the passing of time. Learning the art of pausing is valuable.

43

When you get to the end of the rope,
tie a knot and hang on. And Swing.

Leo Buscaglia

Don't ever, ever, ever give up! You have value, you have gifts, and you have a place in the universe.

Sometimes our grief, loss, or pain is a new beginning. We may not see it at the time, but what's happening to you right now could be in your best interest. For example, maybe you were walking home from the bar with a high level of alcohol in your system and fell down in the snow and passed out. You came to the edge of death, but somehow, someone found you. You received emergency care and were given a second chance. Or maybe you had an automobile accident and spent several months in the hospital and came close to death. Was this a coincidence or a miracle?

Don't take this for granted. You're not a cat with nine lives. Mother Nature always wins in the end. You have been warned. Call it the Great Spirit, the Higher Power, an angel, the Holy Spirit, Budda, Christ, or divine intervention. You lived and you didn't die. This all happened for a reason.

Hang on. Change your life, change your swing and become the person you were meant to be.

44

If a thousand old beliefs were ruined in the march to truth, we must still march on.

Stopford Augustus Brooke

Our belief system comes from our surrounding culture and our family of origin. It tells us what's okay and what's not okay and sets a standard for how we live our lives.

Another great influence with our belief system is advertisement. For example, you can't watch a sporting event without being told how important alcohol is to have fun. What you see and what you hear forms your belief system. Our family of origin also has a great impact on our belief system – what has been role-modeled by Mom, Dad, uncles, aunts, grandparents, cousins, etc.

In finding the truth it's important that we self-examine and take an honest look at who we are and ask ourselves, "What's working and what's not working?" Our true recovery has to do with honesty, asking for help and perseverance.

Be courageous: Seek out a professional counselor or enter a 12 Step program, find a sponsor and really work the steps. Remember, half measures avail us nothing. They simply do not work.

45

We are all like one-winged angels.
It's only when we help each other that we can fly.

Luciano D. Crescenzo

We have to learn to fly. Not run, walk, swim, gallop, but fly. What does this mean? It means we all need to find a path to travel through life full of joy and with peace in our hearts.

Have you ever tried to fly a kite with no tail? Have you ever tried to fly a balsa wood glider with one wing? Have you ever flown a Frisbee that only has one half? It doesn't work! It ends in disaster.

Many of us keep throwing the half-Frisbee, trying to fly the kite with no tail or the airplane with only one wing. Eventually we discover that doing the same thing over and over again doesn't work. If we keep doing what we've always done, we will get what we've always gotten, and that's the sound of a steel door shutting behind us after a change of clothes into the prison uniform of the jail.

Are you ready for change? One key to success and staying out of jail is helping those around you and when you make this a daily habit, that other wing will appear.

People change.

The culture changes,
and more importantly, we change.

There are probably three or more
ways to view or handle any problem.

46

Few things in the world are more powerful than a positive push. A smile. A word of optimism and hope. And you can do it when things are tough.

Richard M. DeVos

Do you know the difference between optimism and pessimism?

There's an old story that I recall about twin boys. One was an optimist and one was a pessimist. When the pessimist was brought to a barn and saw all the horse manure he said, "How terrible! It stinks, it's messy and who is going to clean it up? Why did you bring me here?" When the other twin, the optimist, was brought to the barn and looked around, he said, "Thanks! With all this horse manure there must be a pony around here somewhere," and his heart leapt for joy.

Which one are you? Do you look for the positive in a situation even when the situation seems to be negative? Or do you complain, whine, and cry about how unfairly you've been treated?

Many who have been incarcerated are mad about their present situation saying, "I wouldn't be here if it wasn't for that public defender, judge, district attorney or probation officer!" But the truth of the matter is your personal situation is a gift given to you. It is a time to look within and take a personal inventory.

We cannot see the future but should you choose to take that first step toward change, your gifts and leadership abilities are beyond what you could ever imagine. Be smart, be happy, and make that change that will help you to become who you are meant to be.

47

*I absolutely believe that people if not coached
they never reach their maximum capacity.*

Bob Nardelli

What is a coach? What is a mentor? What is a role model? What is a teacher? All of the above have something in common: They have the ability to bring out the best in us.

One of the things that our higher power wants us to do is our very best with what we have. We are not born equal and we all have different gifts. Some of us can sing and carry a tune and others are tone deaf. One of us might be a great swimmer and another person a great writer. Another may have the capacity to remember everything and yet another might have a poor memory but be very creative.

A mentor or guide in our life could be helpful. They can help us understand who we are and make peace with ourselves even if we aren't the most handsome or prettiest or smartest or most athletic. Coaches appear in many forms or disguises – they may be a teacher, neighbor, co-worker, fellow inmate, jailor, counselor, pastor or even (god forbid!) a probation officer.

Life is not always easy and to go it alone can be very difficult. To do your best should be high on your bucket list so don't hesitate to be coached.

48

*Pursue some path, however narrow and crooked,
in which you can walk with love and reverence.*

Henry David Thoreau

In the movie, *The Wizard of Oz*, Dorothy, the Tin Man, the
Scarecrow and the Lion are told to follow the Yellow Brick Road. At
the end of the road at the Emerald City there would be an all-wise
wizard that would understand their problems and give them what
they needed. Unfortunately, the wizard does not turn out to be as
powerful and knowledgeable as he was made out to be. Dorothy had
more wisdom. She found that change comes from within and said
yes to a different way of understanding and viewing the world.

Some Native Americans talk about the Red Road. Its direction is
similar to Dorothy's wisdom. The Red Road has to do with honesty,
love, helping another, not abusing your body, not abusing another.

When we own our own behavior, only then will things change.
Ask for help and maybe you too can find wisdom and your way
home. Be careful of who you choose as friends, especially of those
who take you down the wrong road. Say to those friends, **gaawiin**,
which simply means, "No," in Ojibwe.

49

Nothing is either good or bad,
but thinking it makes it so.

Shakespeare

I believe there can be good or bad and even what I call gray spots. But the problem is how we view what has happened. Some of us worry or obsess about something that has never happened or will never happen. Fear gets in the way. We think the worst and we don't let go. It becomes part of our being. It is on our mind day and night and we don't sleep well.

I've learned that, "Life is something that happens to us when we're making other plans." We need to do our best and then turn our thoughts over to a higher power. What if we don't have a higher power or a sense of connection to a power greater than ourselves? We're stuck. We continue to ruminate, obsess, and it keeps us from living our lives.

It may be time to find a higher power and the wisdom of the 12 step program and to take one day at a time.

50

*You cannot always control what goes on outside,
but you can always control what goes on inside.*

Wayne Dyer

Most of us get into trouble when we try to change things we can't control. A series of stressful events can make us angry, even fill us with rage.

Learning when to let go can be a difficult thing. We might find ourselves obsessing about little things that if left alone, in time, would work themselves out. But we want what we want and we want it right now!

Someone once said that half of what we worry about never comes true. Worrying is a great thief of time and can ruin an entire day.

There is a philosophy that can help in our daily living. It goes like this:

We're responsible for the effort but not the outcome.

If we feel we have put forth the right energy and have done the right things, if it doesn't turn out the way we want, it probably wasn't meant to be. Most of the time we are powerless over what goes on around us, with people and circumstances. It is possible, however, that with time, practice and patience we can learn to control our reaction and stay out of trouble.

There is a philosophy
that can help in our daily living.

It goes like this:

*We are responsible for the effort
but not the outcome.*

– Ernie Larson –

51

Say not I have found the truth,
but rather I formed a truth.

Kahlil Gibran

A parable tells of guardians in heaven who care for the *Diamond of Truth*. Every day theses guardians would uncover the Diamond of Truth – which was huge, bigger than most houses – and they would polish and shine the diamond. Sometimes a piece of dust from this diamond would fall to the earth and someone would come along and discover that small dust of a diamond and build an institution, a church, or a religion on this small particle of diamond dust and they would exclaim that they had found the whole truth.

I think this is a great story, as it warns us the truth we have today may not be the whole truth.

People change. The culture changes, and more importantly, we change. **There are probably three or more ways to view or handle any problem.**

52

Success consists of going from failure to failure without loss of enthusiasm.

Sir Winston Churchill

Drug and alcohol addiction is cunning, baffling and powerful according to the AA Big Book. This means, should you choose to go through treatment, the average recovering addict takes three to four treatment programs before he or she sustains sobriety.

Don't give up. Perseverance is a word that means stay the course, stick with the program, don't ever give in.

Winston Churchill, a British political leader in World War II, made this point after the end of the war. Churchill was very grateful for the United States and their involvement in WWII. Churchill's country, Great Britain, was devastated – buildings were bombed and mutilated and lives were destroyed. It was a living hell.

Rumor has it that when Winston Churchill gave a speech he took one of his shoes and banged it on the podium for 10 minutes saying, "Never give in, never give in, never, never, never, never." He went on to say, "In nothing, great or small, large or petty, never give in except to convictions of honour and good sense."

You too must never give in. You have special gifts and talents and should you get on the other side of your addiction and "stinkin' thinkin'" (errors in thinking) life will be different. Yes, your life can be restored and rebuilt, just like at the end of World War II with all of its destruction, the Marshall Plan rebuilt Europe.

53

The most difficult thing is the decision to act, the rest is merely tenacity. The fears are paper tigers. You can do anything you decide to do. You can act to change and control your life; and the procedure, the process is its own reward.

Amelia Earhart

A few years ago on the front page of the *Ashland Daily Press* (Ashland, Wisconsin) was a newspaper article titled, "A Daredevil Swim to Devils Island." There were three older men in their late 60's who did a marathon relay swim – 20.3 miles on Lake Superior, from Bayfield, Wisconsin to Devils Island in the Apostle Islands National Lakeshore. They had a support boat and the routine was to swim for one hour, rotate swimmers, and then rest for two hours. It took 10 hours, 37 minutes, 54 seconds to complete the swim. At times the water was calm and flat, at other times strong currents pulled at the swimmers. Lake Superior also delivered a thunderstorm and wind with two to three foot waves.

I was one of those swimmers, and swam six and one-half miles that day. I loved that swim, what an adventure! It was good for my body, mind and spirit. It brought me alive, it gave me purpose. After the swim I thought about this experience and put my words to paper, in a piece called *Life After 60*:

> *When we get older we need to stretch ourselves and move outside of our comfort zone through risk taking with courage, endurance, and perseverance otherwise life becomes boring. We cannot just say life is over and ride into the sunset... Helping others and taking good care of ourselves makes a difference and is a key to having a better life.*

You do not have to be over 60 to honor these truths. We need to learn about stepping outside of our comfort zone to live a better life. We do this by taking the path of courage and perseverance instead of the path of complacency.

No matter our age we can continue to develop our authentic self. Becoming the person we are meant to be has to do with change. If one has an addiction, one needs to have courage to find treatment in some form whether it be counseling, drug court, a sober house, Alcoholics Anonymous (AA), Narcotic Anonymous (NA), etc. We need to risk to change our lifestyle and one effective way to do it, as Amelia Earhart says, is to make the decision to act.

Remember this old saying: "Courage is fear that has said its prayers."

54

The right man is the one who seizes the moment.
Goethe

How many seconds are there in a day? 86,400 seconds. There are many moments during the day when we can say something or say nothing to seize the moment. Sometimes the best way is to shut our mouth. Other times when we see somebody being picked on or discredited, it could be wise to seize the moment and speak up for him or her. This is not easy to do for it's difficult to know when to go and when to stop.

The Serenity Prayer can be a guide, "God grant me the serenity to accept the things I cannot change, the courage to change the things I can, and the wisdom to know the difference."

We waste our time, talent and energy when we try to change something that can't be changed. It's like backing up ten feet away from a concrete wall and then taking a running start and slamming our head into the wall. The wall is not going to move and often change comes in waiting for the right moment or talking to the right person, or in saying nothing and surrendering ourselves to the silence of our higher power.

Some Native Americans
talk about the Red Road.

It has to do with

honesty,

love,

helping another,

not abusing your body,

and not abusing another.

55

The first principle of success is desire –
knowing what you want.
Desire is the planting of the seed.

Robert Collier

Do you really know what you want in life?   Do you know what will make you happy?   Do you love yourself as you are?   What are your desires?   What are your wants?   What are your needs?   Take some time today to answer those questions.   Take a pencil and piece of paper and journal your thoughts.

Success in life rests in making the right personal decisions.   For many of us, we have been plagued with bad choices and their consequences and we continue to live a lifestyle of this behavior over and over and over again, until we believe this is who we really are even if it's hurtful to us and everyone around us.

If you want to change, start small by doing little acts of kindness – be non-judgmental, loving and giving in small ways just for the day. The bottom line is, what we really want in life is to love and be loved and it all begins with the right kind of thinking.   Plant the seeds of change with the desire to stay sober and clean, with compassionate honesty as your benchmark to success.

56

Dreams grow holy when put into action.

Adelaide Ann Proctor

Many of us feel like we are victims of society. We grew up in bad neighborhoods, dysfunctional families, abusive childhoods, and in a school system that didn't work for us. We say, "It's not my fault and I survived in the best way I could." But you know deep down inside that there is a dream to be put into action. You know that there can be a better life and it's time to say, "I don't want this old life anymore."

The 12 Step program has a slogan, originally from Shakespeare **To thy own self be true**. We know when we are manipulating or playing the con game. As long as we continue to cling to our untruths or bad habits that aren't life-enhancing, we rob ourselves of our birth right and God-given gifts.

Today, find a vision and a purpose that is good – one that helps others and you. Stop the drug and alcohol abuse. Stop the self-abuse. Stop the manipulation. Stop the "poor me" attitude.

Stop taking what doesn't belong to you. Find your dream, breathe, and take action.

57

*You are successful the moment you start
moving toward a worthwhile goal.*

Chuck Carlson

What is success? When you were a child, was success getting an A on your spelling test, or was it just getting a passing grade? Was it playing on the Little League baseball team and being the star player, or was it just making the team? If you've ever run a marathon you don't have to win because winning comes in training and running the race.

There are 7.5 billion people on the planet and many of them are going to perform better than you, and many will perform worse than you, so go slow and be kind to yourself. It's important to be true to yourself to find the real you.

Goals are important. **Shoot for the stars, but if you land on the moon, you've done well.** And remember, success starts with having goals, no matter how small.

Take action for success one step at a time.

58

It is one of the beautiful compensations of this life that no man can sincerely help another without helping himself.

Ralph Waldo Emerson

How many times have we heard that we are the ones that benefit when we reach out to another?   I have learned over the years by sharing my story, pain and loss, I give another permission to risk and share their pain and deep hurt. Sharing is an important step toward healing.

We are not all bad. Just because some of us have made bad choices doesn't make us evil. I have heard many alcoholics say after their third or fourth DWI and having to serve several months incarcerated, "We're not criminals, we're alcoholics." This is true and not true.

When we make a poor choice and cross the line or violate society's boundaries where we can cause hurt or pain for someone, then there must be consequences or punishment. We need change and that has to do with a lifestyle change, which consists of asking for help, getting honest, making amends, and finding sobriety. Once we have achieved sobriety we can then help another.

The Prayer of St. Francis of Assissi (page B10) says, **It's in giving that we receive.** It has become a true cliché; indeed, by helping another we help ourselves.

59

First you jump off the cliff and
build wings on the way down.

Having faith in what we don't see is optional. In the third Indiana
Jones movie, *Indiana Jones and the Last Crusade,* Indiana Jones is
asked to step out into thin air and walk across an invisible bridge.
Any sane person would say, "What a fool!" Stepping out over the
abyss was sure death; but Indiana Jones believed the bridge would
appear and it did.

For now you cannot see how your life will be different, but it
will. Talk to any old-timer in a Narcotics Anonymous or Alcoholics
Anonymous 12 Step program who has significant years of sobriety.
They will tell you how bridges have appeared when they had faith,
how their shoulders have broadened, or how their wingspan has
increased when in difficult times.

Your wings will grow when you choose to live a healthy lifestyle.
Surely if you continue to do what you've always done, one of three
things will happen: illness, death, or a long stay in your county jail or
state prison.

Take a chance – one cannot change without faith. Change comes
through courage with a journey to the center of your self.

Success consists of
going from failure to failure
without loss of enthusiasm.

– Sir Winston Churchill –

60

You weren't an accident. You weren't mass produced. You aren't an assembly line product. You are deliberately planned, specifically gifted and lovingly positioned on earth by the master craftsman.

Max Lucado

We are living, breathing and loving human beings ever if we are incarcerated. For some of us it isn't until we are locked up, stopped in our tracks, sick or ill that we become aware of our need to change.

Incarceration can give us time to think and reposition the direction of our life. It may take several sentences of lock-up before we actually make this shift in consciousness. During this time we search our mind and soul and sometimes we get a glimpse of what we could become.

We are entitled to the pursuit of happiness. Debra Frasier, a children's book author says, "On the day you were born a forest of tall trees collected the sun's light in their leaves where, in silent mystery, they made oxygen for you to breathe..."

Take time today to discover who you really are and what you want. You have gifts and you have purpose – when you ask for help from another human being or your higher power the direction of your life will change.

61

Clarity is purpose.

Buckminster Fuller

Part of the problem in living our lives is when we have no purpose and lack direction in life. When we connect with our same old friends who live by poor values, we become like a leaf in the wind. If the wind blows north, we go north. If the wind is blowing south, we go south. What contributes to the problem of having no purpose or direction is the misuse of our energy by turning to drugs and alcohol, sex, and poor choices to recharge ourselves.

The spiritual leaders of the world suggest that we do God's will, that we find meaningful purpose in life. The four most dreaded words in our society are, "God's will be done." We are doubtful of this phrase as we want full control of our life. However, if your life is one of darkness and imprisonment, it's time to take a risk and find direction that brings forth your purpose – your wisdom, your ideals, your gifts and your dreams.

62

Believe and act as if it were impossible to fail.

Charles Kettering

We give up so easily. This can become a learned character defect. If things don't go exactly the way we want them to go, we abandon ship when maybe we were doing the right thing, but at the wrong time, or in the wrong place or with the wrong person. The solution lies with staying with it. Perseverance is never giving up. Yes, there are times that we need to ask for direction and to, **Let go and let God.**

Author M. Scott Peck wrote the book, *The Road Less Traveled*. The book was on the New York Times Best Seller List for several years. However, this book sat in the warehouse for five years before it was discovered and made the best seller list!

Sometimes our timing is not the Creator's timing. Be patient. Do good deeds, love others, and believe and act as if it is impossible for you to fail.

63

*There are only two days in the year that nothing can be done. One is called **yesterday** and the other is called **tomorrow**, so today is the right day to love, believe, do, and mostly live.*

Dalai Lama

There are times in our lives when we make poor choices and wish we could go back and have a do-over. Well, we all know that is not possible. As some may say, "It is water under the bridge," meaning what was said, action taken, or mistakes made are all history. We only have today, and tomorrow is not yet here.

Bill Wilson's 12 Step Program, Alcoholics Anonymous, provides a way that can be helpful, useful and healing. In Step 9 it says that we need to own our mistakes and make amends when possible (except when to do so would injure you or others), and ask for direction for the Universe (God) for tomorrow when it comes.

Be kind, be forgiving, believe in yourself and do not be afraid to ask for help for you are not alone. We need to ***ask... ask... ask...*** and remember this: The Universe wants you to be happy, to live, love and have confidence in what you do.

It is time to make that long overdue change. The truth is, you are somebody and you deserve good things in your life: Like a job you enjoy, a home, a car, a spouse, children who will love you, money, friends, and good health.

Sobriety should be our number one goal. Be wise and surround yourself with people who want you to have a good life – ***just for today, and one day at a time***.

64

Every act of kindness has a positive ripple effect with no end, not only with our hands but with our hearts and souls we can bless the lives of others.

Scott Adams

You don't have to be in prison to feel the pain of incarceration. This can be done foolishly by the powerlessness of addiction to the drug of your choice. Change almost always needs to start from the inside out. It can begin by practicing compassion daily. Mark Twain once said, "Kindness is a language that the deaf can hear and the blind can see."

Has your addiction blocked you from becoming the person you were meant to be? For today, try not to judge but substitute a word of kindness for every word of negativity (this can be done with your thoughts too!). 12-step programs have slogans... one of them is "ACT AS IF". It is a great tool to shift from negative to positive thinking, or fake it 'til you make it.

If you practice daily that you are a kind, caring, giving person, soon that will become your reality. It can and will help you find a way out of the false belief that the drug of your choice is your friend. Be aware that your thoughts become your teachers. The bottom line is, we need to learn tolerance rooted in love, or simply said, "Be kind, loving and have compassion."

Kindness is a language
the deaf can hear
and the blind can see.

– Mark Twain –

65

*Mainly what meditation has been teaching me is to
listen, listen, listen to everything going on around me.
It works slowly, but it works. Every spiritual tradition
around the world has its own practice of meditation.
Prayer for me is the act of reaching out to God.
Meditation is being still and listening to God. "*

Tom Linnell, EdD

The 11th step of the Big Book of AA says we need to improve our conscious contact with God through prayer and meditation, asking for direction, strength and power. Most of us know something about prayer but what do we know about meditation? It's often overlooked and not discussed.

What we do know is that there is a direct link between self-examination, prayer and meditation, each to be taken seriously and separately. Learning to meditate opens our mind to a higher power. Here we learn to relax, become quiet and still. Our thinking (often obsessive and racing thoughts) slows down. We move away from self-pity, self-seeking and dishonesty.

Meditation can help when we are stressed. It's a place you can go at almost anytime to be renewed and find strength to deal with life's problems. The word "meditation" comes from the Latin verb, "meditari", meaning to reflect upon. Meditation is not a religion, so it doesn't interfere with personal spiritual beliefs. It strengthens your basic goodness and reconnects you with your true authentic self.

There are many styles or ways to meditate. I suggest you experiment with different methods and their practices. When you become committed to one practice, it can become a lifelong skill.

Here are a few options to explore:

- Mindfulness Meditation
- Breathing Meditation
- Loving Kindness Meditation
- St. Ignatius Meditation,
- Body Scan Meditation,
- Walking Meditation
- Basic Concentration Meditation
- Stretching Meditation
- Centering Prayer
- Communion with Nature
- Reading 12-Steps or scripture
- etc.

For more information on meditation see Appendix C on page 108.

66

Having ADHD is like having a powerful race car for a brain, but with bicycle brakes. Treating ADHD is like strengthening your brakes, so you start to win races in your life.

Dr. Edward Hallowell

Responding to my questions about ADD and ADHD with adults in rehab or in jail settings, psychologist and addictions counselor Dr. Tom Linnell offered this valuable information:

People come to rehab for addictions, but it frequently turns out they also have an untreated attention-deficit disorder (ADD) or attention-deficit/hyperactivity disorder (ADHD).

We have been around the block in the last 20 or 30 years in this country in diagnosing ADD/ADHD, including questions about how many adults still suffer from it. My experience at the rehab center is that the disorder affects our clients at a higher rate than in the general population. Many times these adults have never been diagnosed accurately, or, if diagnosed, have not been treated successfully.

*We have learned that when the disorder is identified and treated, the individual is less likely to relapse after returning to the community. Effective treatment usually includes both education about ADD/ADHD and the prescription of a carefully selected, non-addictive medication, like **Strattera**.*

When the disorder is not treated, individuals relapse at a rate much higher than average, often with fatal consequences.

The common symptoms of the disorder – impulsivity, disorganization, poor attention span – contribute to poor decisions at critical moments in the recovery process. When the disorder is treated correctly, individuals have a much better chance to sustain their recovery program over the long haul.

I know that rehab centers and correctional setting have a lot in common, and the problem of ADD/ADHD is very likely a major challenge for both. The good news is that proper diagnosis and treatment can be made available in both settings, saving lives and reducing the costs of relapse at the same time.

The God in the universe wants you to be happy, wants you to express your gifts, wants you to live,

67

love and have confidence in what you do.

Author Unknown

On June 10th in 1935, in Akron, Ohio, William Wilson and Bob Smith formed a recovery program known as Alcoholics Anonymous. It was based on the six principles of the Oxford Group. Its formula was, admit hopelessness, get honest with yourself, get honest with another, make amends, help others without demand, and pray to Christ (to God, a higher power, or the power of possibility).

The Oxford Group, founded in 1921, was a Christian organization lead by a Christian missionary, Dr. Frank Buchman, who believed that the root of all problems was based on fear and selfishness. In today's world a well-educated therapist would look towards ***traumas*** related to rejection, abandonment, and/or betrayal.

In the early days of Alcoholics Anonymous there was a division and controversy over the word "God". For many the word God was tied to traditional religious ways. Many were atheist (not believing) or agnostic (not sure). What evolved was a compromise suggesting a power greater than ourselves or a personal spiritual relationship.

The 12-steps are a recovery program which does not assign a belief system, but makes room for each person's unique spiritual perspective. **Addiction** is a **spiritual disease**. The beginning of recovery is the admission that we are powerless, that there is a power greater than ourselves, and that we turn it over and ask for help.

When you do the right thing you become connected to that power and good things happen.

68

If you are bored with life and if you don't get up in the morning with a burning desire to do things, you don't have enough goals.

Lou Holtz
legendary NCAA football coach

Part of the problem for many of us is that we are bored with life. We have stimulated ourselves with drugs, alcohol and dishonest behaviors. We have gone into relationships that match our thinking or our values and over time, they do not work out.

Locked away in our own pain of depression and anxiety we do not want to get up in the morning and we do not care. Some who are incarcerated count the days, others do not and do not care and their thinking continues to be dishonest. You may say to yourself, "Next time I won't get caught!", or "Drugs and alcohol are not a problem for me."

Within a day, a week, a month after our release we become bored. We go back to our old friends and places we have hung out and soon the drug that keeps you from becoming the person you are meant to be is back in your body. It is the three Ps that kept you connected to your old life: your **playthings**, your **playmates**, and your **playground**. Staying away from your playthings (drugs and alcohol) is not enough, the other two Ps will bring you back to your addiction as well.

Upon release from incarceration you have to learn a new way. Find new goals, get outdoors and walk three or four times a week for 20 to 30 minutes, and find new and healthy friends. If you don't change, nothing changes. Remember, what you want starts with you.

69

My goal is to empower others to move beyond their limitations and live their dreams.

Lori Schneider

In the summer of 2009 I had the pleasure of meeting Lori Schneider, who had just climed Mount Everest. I had a gathering on the front porch of my house and had invited five people – two psychologists, a newspaper writer, Lori Schneider and myself.

I wish I had recorded our conversations that day while we talked and enjoyed coffee and scones between words. Lori's story of climbing Mount Everest was incredible, extraordinary, and inspiring. It was not just about the physical climb, but her deep commitment to overcome the disability bestowed upon her and finding a higher purpose in what looked like a slow death sentence.

In 1999 at age 43 Lori Schneider woke one morning with numbness in 50% of her body. In a very short time it had spread throughout her entire body. The diagnosis was the crippling disease of Multiple Sclerosis. The news of having this auto-immune disorder left her with fear that her physical life as she knew it would end and her future would be a life confined to a wheelchair. Lori chose to dramatically change her life as she knew it. She left a 22 year marriage, quit a 20 year teaching career, sold her house and moved away from friends and community.

R. D. Laing, a Scottish psychiatrist, once said, "A crazy act in a crazy situation is really sane." Lori found herself in such a situation and decided to accelerate her love of travel and the mountains to climb the highest peak on each continent. She became the first person in the world with Multiple Sclerosis to conquer the seven summits of the world.

On May 23, 2009 Lori climbed her last highest peak, Mount Everest at 29,035 feet. For Lori, climbing had a higher purpose, one which would carry the light of hope and a message of strength to those who face insurmountable odds. She believes that we need to go beyond our fear and pain, to persevere, "If we believe, we can achieve."

Climbing has taught Lori how important it is to believe in yourself, even when others do not. She says,

> Live your dreams and take risks – you have to get out there sometimes and dreaming in your life and take the steps you need to make it happen. We can find courage and strength from within, it is what gets you to the summit of mountains and to the summit of your life.

After completing her final summit, mountain climber Lori Schneider went on to be an author, educator, life-long learner, international motivational speaker, and most important of all, a global advocate for all those living with neurological disorders and disabilities.

Whatever fears, doubts and misfortune is in your life take a risk.

Believe in yourself and dream big.

70

Nie m'oj cyrk, nie moje malpy.
translation: Not my circus, not my monkeys.

Polish Proverb

My brother and I were talking about a mutual friend that was making poor choices. During our conversation I suggested what I thought were some practical solutions to these problems. My brother came back with this statement, "Not my circus, not my monkeys." I stopped in mid-protest and started laughing. **He was right!!** My "Jedi training" developed a need to try and fix everyone's problems; this extended into my life professionally and personally. There was a lot of meaning in that simple phrase.

Many of us devote our energy into thinking and talking over problems in which we have no control. Now, don't get we wrong. It's not a bad thing to be there for others; however, sometimes the best way to help others, family and friends included, is to let them **help themselves**.

A well-known psychiatrist and friend, Foster W. Cline, MD, has written several books on parenting and has lectured all over the planet. He presented original concepts in 1990 that addressed, "Whose problem is whose problem?" and "Helicopter parenting," that suggest that the caretakers of children and adolescents stay over-involved instead of staying out of the way.

Cline said that we actually hurt our kids by not letting them solve their own problems, unless of course the issue is related to life or limb. This also applies to adults in the home, community and workplace.

It is important that we develop the skill of excusing ourselves from other people's circuses (problems) so we can get back to our own life and our own business. It means that we don't get emotionally involved in a problem and even sometimes end an argument by refusing to participate. We all have the right to remain silent and walk away from a potentially toxic situation. As a 12-Step program slogan states, "Let go and let God," and detach with love.

Grace is a love which has nothing to do with us,

but everything to do with the one

from whom it is derived: God.

It is a powerful, divine and vital piece

of our existence, and it is the only reason

we are able to open our eyes each morning.

God's grace is more than a second chance;

it's a third, fourth and fifth chance.

It's a love that keeps on giving,

regardless of our past.

Appendix A – A.A. Materials

The A.A. Promises

If we are painstaking about this phase of our development, we will be amazed before we are half way through. We are going to know a new freedom and a new happiness. We will not regret the past nor wish to shut the door on it. We will comprehend the word serenity and we will know peace. No matter how far down the scale we have gone, we will see how our experience can benefit others. That feeling of uselessness and self-pity will disappear. We will lose interest in selfish things and gain interest in our fellows. Self-seeking will slip away. Our whole attitude and outlook upon life will change. Fear of people and of economic insecurity will leave us. We will intuitively know how to handle situations which used to baffle us. We will suddenly realize that God is doing for us what we could not do for ourselves.

Are these extravagant promises? We think not. They are being fulfilled among us – sometimes quickly, sometimes slowly. They will always materialize if we work for them.

Big Book, Alcoholics Anonymous (pp. 83-84).

The 12 Steps

Guide for Living

1. We admitted we were powerless over certain areas of our lives – that our lives had become unmanageable.

Alcoholics Anonymous

1. We admitted we were powerless over alcohol – that our lives had become unmanageable.

2. Came to believe that a Power greater than ourselves could restore us to sanity.

3. Made a decision to turn our will and our lives over to the care of God as we understood Him.

4. Made a searching and fearless moral inventory of ourselves.

5. Admitted to God, to ourselves and to another human being the exact nature of our wrongs.

6. Were entirely ready to have God remove all these defects of character.

7. Humbly asked Him to remove our shortcomings.

8. Made a list of all persons we had harmed, and became willing to make amends to them all.

9. Made direct amends to such people wherevers possible, except when to do so would injure them or others.

10. Continued to take personal inventory and when we were wrong promptly admitted it.

11. Sought through prayer and meditation to improve our conscious contact with God as we understood Him, praying only for knowledge of His will for us and the power to carry that out.

12. Having had a spiritual awakening as the result of these steps, we tried to carry this message to others and to practice these principles in all our affairs.

12. Having had a spiritual awakening as the result of these steps, we tried to carry this message to alcoholics and to practice these principles in all our affairs.

Founded by Ernie Larson, in Minneapolis Minnesota, February 13, 1974

Appendix B – Prayers

3rd Step Prayer

God, I offer myself to Thee – to build me and to do with me as thou will. Relieve me of the bondage of self, that I may better do Thy will. Take away my difficulties, that victory over them may bear witness to those I would help of Thy Power, Thy Love, and Thy Way of Life. May I do Thy will always!

Big Book, Alcoholics Anonymous (p. 63).

Seventh Step Prayer

My Creator, I am now willing that you should have all of me, the good and the bad. I pray that you remove from me every single defect of my character which stands in the way of my usefulness to You and my fellows, and grant me strength, as I go out from here, to do Your bidding. Amen.

Big Book, Alcoholics Anonymous (p. 76).

Serenity Prayer
official short version

As adopted by A.A.

God grant me the serenity to accept the things I cannot change,

Courage to change the things I can, and

Wisdom to know the difference.

Serenity Prayer
original version: complete, unabridged

by Reinhold Niebuhr (1892-1971)

God, give us grace to accept with serenity
The things that cannot be changed,
Courage to change the things
which should be changed,
and the Wisdom to distinguish
the one from the other.

Living one day at a time,
Enjoying one moment at a time,
Accepting hardship as a pathway to peace,
Taking, as Jesus did,
This sinful world as it is,
Not as I would have it,
Trusting that You will make all things right,

If I surrender to Your will,
So that I may be reasonably happy in this life,
And supremely happy with You forever in the next.
Amen.

Serenity Prayer in Ojibwe Language

Translated into Ojibwe by Rick Gresczyk and Jim Clark

Gichi Manidoo

daga wiidookawishin

weweni

ji naanaagadawendamaan

ji odaapinamaan

iniw ge – gashkitoosiwaan

ji aanjisidooyaan

ji de – apiichide' eyaan

ji aanjisidooyaan

ge-gashkitooyaan

ji-de-appiichinibwaakaayaan

ji gikendamaan ono

Prayers from *24 Hours A Day*

A Prayer to Stay Out of Trouble

I pray that I may submit to the laws of nature and to the laws of God, I pray that I may live in harmony with all the laws of life.

A Prayer of Sacrifice and All Suffering

I pray that I may accept pain and defeat as part of God's plan for my spiritual growth.

A Prayer for a Simple Life

I pray that I may love the simple things in life. I pray I may keep my life uncomplicated and free.

A Prayer for Good Things

I pray that whatever is good I may have. I pray that I may leave to God the choice of what good will come to me.

Prayer for Loving Others and Self

I pray that I may do all I can to love others, in spite of their many faults. I pray that as I love, so I be loved.

Reflection of God's Will

I pray that I may try to be a reflection of Divine Light. I pray that some of its rays may shine in my life.

A Prayer for Abundant Living

I pray that I may live to give. I pray that I may learn this secret of abundant living (help me to give of my time, talent and treasure).

The Universal Prayer

Eternal Reality,
You are Everywhere.

You are Infinite Unity, Truth and Love;
You permeate our souls,
Every corner of the Universe and beyond.

To some of us You are Father, Friend, or Partner
To others, Higher Power, Higher Self, or Inner self.
To many of us You are all of these and more.
You are within us and we within You.

We know You forgive our trespasses
If we forgive ourselves and others.
We know You protect us from destructive temptation
If we continue to seek Your help and guidance.
We know You provide us food and shelter today
If we but place our trust in You and try to do our best.
Give us this day knowledge of Your will for us and the
        power to carry it out.
For Yours is Infinite Power and Love, Forever

The Lord's Prayer

Our Father, who art in Heaven

Hallowed be Thy name.

Thy kingdom come.

Thy Will be done on earth as it is in Heaven.

Give us this day our daily bread,

And forgive us our trespasses, as we forgive those who trespass against us.

Lead us not into temptation, but deliver us from evil.

For Thine is the Kingdom

And the Power

And the Glory

Forever.

Amen.

Prayer of Gratitude, Blessings and Temptation

Help me Creator Spirit, to resist all of the temptations of this day. Give me the inner strength to turn away, to face the light of recovery, and to trust myself to take the right path for me. Help me to breathe, to stand tall, to recognize my many blessings, and to realize all I have in my life, and all I stand to lose. I ask this humbly from you, for you know the true person inside of me – my strengths and weaknesses. They blend to make up the person I am. Help me to recognize the real power I have and how I can use that power to serve you, others in my life, and to find true happiness.

Praying for the Enemy

By Morton Kelsey, *Caring: How Can We Love One Another?*

This is a Christian prayer of intercession. The best method of praying in a general way for other people is to pray the Lord's Prayer for them. If "Tom" is the one I am praying for, say:

Tom's father who art in heaven, hallowed be thy name in Tom. Thy kingdom come in Tom, Thy will be done in Tom, on earth just as if he were with you in heaven. Give him his daily bread, all that he needs to sustain and enrich his life. Forgive Tom and help him to forgive himself and others. Do not put Tom to the test as he is weak like the rest of us, and please deliver Tom from the evil one. Let Tom's joy be in Your kingdom and power and glory forever and ever.

Pray for the Gift of Change

by T.P. Faust

Author of all things that watches over us, God of the sun, the moon, the sky, the trees, the rocks, the water, and all living things, grant to me what is good and stable in my life. I am sick and tired of my old habits and poor choices. I am not capable of change without your help. Please grace me with your power and wisdom and those you send my way who will direct, encourage and teach me to not fear or resist a new start or new way of life. For without change there can be no true meaning to my life.

Morning Prayer for Guidance

from the text, A Course in Miracles
published by the Foundation for Inner Peace

Say this prayer and then listen for guidance and wisdom, "What would you have me do today? Where would you have me go? What would you have me say, and to whom?

Prayer of Saint Francis of Assisi

Lord, make me an instrument of thy peace!

That where there is hatred, I may bring love.

That where there is wrong, I may bring the spirit
of forgiveness.

That where there is discord, I may bring harmony.

That were there is error, I may bring truth.

That were there is doubt, I may bring faith.

That where there is despair, I may bring hope.

That were there are shadows, I may bring light.

That where there is sadness, I may bring joy.

Lord, grant that I may seek rather to comfort,
than to be comforted.

To understand, than to be understood.

To love, than to be loved.

For it is in giving that we recieve.

It is by forgiving that one is forgiven.

It is by dying that one awakens to Eternal Life.

Prayer for Blessings and Recovery

by Anonymous

Creator Spirit, thank you for my many gifts and blessings. Guide me in sharing them with those around me. By directing my energy for good, I stay on the path to recovery. My past is just that – passed. By letting go of the shame and anger I can then direct that strong energy into a life source for good. Help me to work toward positive experiences and alliances – ones which won't compromise my reputation ever again – ones which will enhance my relationship with those who love me and care about me – ones which will bring real happiness and contentment to me. With this prayer, I symbolically release the errors of my wrongdoings, shame, and pain of the past, and I renew my efforts to work toward a healthy and joyful future.

Selichah

Jewish prayer asking for forgiveness

Blessing Six of the Amidah

Forgive us, our Father, for we have sinned; pardon us, our King, for we have rebelled; for you are a pardoner and a forgiver. Blessed are you, Lord, the gracious one who abundantly forgives.

Refuah

Jewish prayer asking for healing

Blessing Eight of the Amidah

Heal us, O Lord, and we shall be healed; save us, and we will be
saved, for the one we praise is You. Bring complete healing for all
our sicknesses, O God, for You are our faithful and compassionate
Healer and King. Blessed are you, Lord, the Healer of the sick (of
Israel).

Buddhist Daily Affirmation Prayer

Namu Amida Buddha.

Entrusting in the Primal Vow of Buddha,

Calling out the Buddha-name,

I shall pass through the journey of life with strength and joy.

Revering the Light of Buddha,

Reflecting upon my imperfect self,

I shall proceed to live a life of gratitude.

Following the Teachings of Buddha,

Listening to the Right Path,

I shall share the True Dharma with all.

Rejoicing in the compassion of Buddha,

Respecting and aiding all sentient beings,

I shall work towards the welfare of society and the world.

Appendix C – Meditation

Notes on Learning to Meditate

by Tom Linnell, Psychologist, EdD

The goal of meditation is a peaceful mind. The path toward the goal can be found by stopping and paying attention. This is often called "mindfulness."

Start by sitting down. This stops the usual rush to be getting things done. (About sitting. It turns out that standing, walking and even lying down can work just as well. Most of us begin with sitting and try out the other postures later.)

Find a sitting position that is stable and relaxing. This could be cross-legged on a pillow, straight up in a chair, semi-kneeling on a low bench, or another position you find for yourself.

Sit still. Not rigid, just quiet.

If your sitting posture is uncomfortable, you will not like it. Your mind will not become more peaceful. With practice, you will discover sitting positions that feel stable and comfortable. May meditators appreciate the value of keeping their spines straight. (Something about a straight spine makes it easier to let go of thoughts and emotions and develop greater clarity of mind.)

You may close your eyes, or let them rest half-open, gazing on a place just in front of you. Many people like having a small object out there to focus on, like a candle or a flower or a stone.

Then, follow your breathing. Breathing in, be aware of your breathing in; breathing out, be aware of your breathing out. In, out.

Your breathing may be shallow and fast when you are stressed, and deeper and slower when you relax.

It is not necessary to try to change your breathing. Let it be.

This is a point where most meditators begin to notice their distractions – an itch, a thought about a chore, irritation at a noisy dog, an urge to get up and do something. This is the good stuff, the very stuff that prompted you to start meditating in the first place. You have it right there in your immediate experience. Now what?

What to do about the distractions that rob you of a peaceful mind? Let them come. Let them go. Breathe in, breathe out. In, out.

Notice what comes up for you. Concentrate on it if you need to, and then let it go.

Breathe.

Your body and your mind will hint to you when you have meditated enough at one time. For most people, this can vary from five minutes to a half an hour, depending on the day. Try out what seems to work for you.

You may also enjoy meditating while walking. Try it. Walk at a calm pace, one that lets you enjoy the contact between your foot and the ground. Let your breath flow in and out in time with your steps. You can practice repeating a short phrase in time with your steps and your breathing. Perhaps, "Be here now; be here now; be here now."

When you hurry, you focus more on where you are going than where you actually are. Or else, your mind goes someplace else completely. Meditation means really being exactly where you are, with your mind and body together.

Walking often exposes us to lots more distractions – sights, sounds, smells, sensations, movements of other people, the constant possibility of the unexpected.

And your mind will still want to play with the old distractions, too. What to do? Let them come, let them go. Breathe in, breathe out. Move quietly on your path.

Once you have started practicing meditation, you will probably ask yourself whether you are "doing it right." It may help to talk with other people who are learning to meditate, to appreciate the variety of people's experiences.

It will definitely help to remind yourself that there is no one "right" way.

Ask, share, practice some more. Find the way that brings your mind peace, and take that path one mindful step at a time.

Appendix D
Tips for an
Authentic Life

HALT before you leap.

Ask yourself:

    Am I **H**ungry?
    Am I **A**ngry?
    Am I **L**onely?
    Am I **T**ired?

Courage plus perseverance equals miracles.

Addictions steal your spiritual gifts...

and prevent you from honoring your true self.

If you go back to the same **playthings, playmates** & **playgrounds** *you will surely go back to your old ways.*

Relax, reflect, or meditate.

Commit yourself for 10 minutes every day.

Stay prepared.

Yet remain flexible, as *life is what happens when you're busy making other plans.*

There are at least 3 ways of doing anything.

Own your mistakes.

Admit them. Ask...
How can I make it right?
How can I make amends?

Always do your best.

Work with what you have and where you are... *and be grateful.*

Practice daily kindness.

Say something nice. Help someone in need.

When a desire is not met it may not always be a *denial*. It may simply mean *delay*.

You are responsible for the *effort*, not the outcome.

– E. Larsen

Negative people aren't that way because of you.

The "crazymakers," most often have nothing to do with you. Walk away. Take a Zen pass.

[see Reading #2 on page 4]

Prayer is a way to ask for guidance.

Ask your higher power, be it God, Great Spirit, The Christ, The Universe, or the power of possibility.

What we live with, we learn and what we learn, we practice. What we practice, we become. What we become has consequences.

– E. Larsen

Appendix E – Life Map

Living Your Authentic Life Map

The diagram on the next page explains how someone can get off and back on their authentic path.

When we are born into the world genetics and environment play important roles. At birth we are given genetic gifts, which emerge throughout our authentic life.

At the core of our soul is spiritual serenity. If we are betrayed, abandoned, or rejected (physically or emotionally), we feel pain and look for relief. In the *Cupboard of Coping and Relief* we can find a healthy path, in line with our authentic self, – or we may find an unhealthy path. Those who find an unhealthy approach usually stumble on one that is similar to the path of a parent, friend, or sibling.

Once we start on an **un**healthy path we might make some good choices in response to new events. However, we often make more bad choices by going back to what seemed to work for us in the past. Repeating this over and over leads to habitual behavoir. For some it leads to a lifestyle of negative addiction.

At the core of the negative addiction is a false sense of serenity, a belief that this is the true self. It robs us of our gifts and sense of purpose and can cause depression and anxiety. This lifestyle is a spiritual lie. It is formed from a false sense of self and moves us towards death and destruction.

Many things can help restore the authentic self:
- *self examination*
- *good therapy*
- *service to others*
- *self help groups (N.A. and A.A, for example)*
- *other life-changing possibilities (for example, exercise, healthy diet, meditation, creative endeavors, appropriate medication, etc.).*

Living in orange clothes may create an opportunity to retrieve your authentic self.

For more on this see reading #23.

Living Your Authentic Life
A GUIDE FOR GETTING BACK TO WHO YOU REALLY ARE

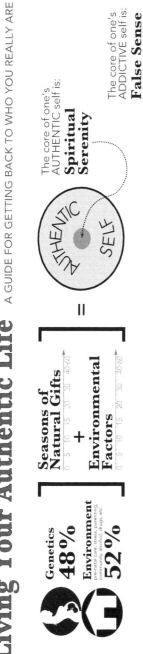

What makes you who you are

Genetics **48%**

Environment **52%**
pre-natal care, stress, parenting, community, alcohol, drugs, etc.

Seasons of Natural Gifts
0 5 10 15 20 30 40-60
+
Environmental Factors
0 5 10 15 20 30 40-60

=

The core of one's AUTHENTIC self is:
Spiritual Serenity

AUTHENTIC SELF

The core of one's ADDICTIVE self is:
False Sense of Security

ADDICTIVE SELF

leads to

DESTRUCTION AND DEATH

THE ADDICTION LIFESTYLE
- A belief that this is the authentic self
- Robs us of our gifts
- Filled with depression and anxiety
- Rooted in a spiritual lie

What gets you off your center

Emotional Traumas
Betrayal
Abandonment
Rejection

PAIN WHICH LEADS TO

leads to seeking help from the
Cupboard of Relief

Healthy	Unhealthy
Medications	Abuse of Drugs and Alcohol
Nutrition	Junk Food
Touch and Nurturing	Bad Touch
Process Anger	Explosive Anger
Nurturing Sex	Obsessive Sex

LEADS TO SOME **RELIEF**

THEN LATER...
NEW EVENTS
OFTEN LEAD TO MORE **PAIN**

If unhealthy actions were taken earlier, new stressful events probably lead to...

RELAPSE
When this repeats it usually becomes

HABIT

What gets you back on center

Self Examination
REFLECT • LOOK WITHIN • QUESTION

Good Therapy
TALK THROUGH FEELINGS

Service to Others
STRETCH OUTSIDE YOURSELF

Self-help Groups
SHARE • LEARN • TEACH

Orange Clothing
USE YOUR TIME WISELY

Created by Timothy P. Faust © 2018
Designed and edited by Will Pipkin
of Copy That, Ashland, Wisconsin

113

Acknowledgements

I dedicate this book to all who have guided me and helped me find my authentic self: my parents, Michael and Dorothy Faust; my brothers, Michael, Kenneth and William; my wife, Heidi Van Dunk; my children, Ryan and Austin; my life teachers Albert Mirand (high school coach), Alexander Bassin (professor of criminology), Foster W. Cline, MD (friend and colleague) Tom Linnell, Ed D (friend and colleague), Jerry Peterson (friend), June Amen (friend), and the inmates of the Bayfield County Jail. Thank you for all you have done for me – you have helped me to become the person I am today.

I deeply appreciate the gifts of my friend and journalist, Barbara Brown. I acknowledge the vital help with design and editing I received from Will Pipkin and others at Copy That, located in Ashland, Wisconsin.

Timothy P. Faust

I acknowledge with grace and love my mother and father, Evelyn and Kenneth Brown, and my beloved sister Patricia Brown who would have been very pleased with the purpose and publication of this book, and my brothers Dennis and Scott Brown and dear friends Linda Krehbiel, France Austin Miller, Susan Brown and Jana Van Evera for their ongoing encouragement to see this book into print.

Barbara A. Brown

Manuscript Reviews

The lessons in this book are meaningful. The problem is people need to change in order to want to read this book and become their new self.

Bernie Siegel, M.D.

I just finished reading "Soul Retrieval: Reclaiming Your Authentic Life". I can't imagine a book would be more helpfull to inmates or individuals with addictive or substance abuse problems. Considering the fact there are several million people incarcerated and have an addiction problem this book could change lives. Every page has something meaningful, worthwhile, powerful, or memorable.

Foster W. Cline, M.D.
Founder, with Jim Fay, of
Love and Logic, Inc.

I'm not in recovery from drugs or an inmate looking to find a path. I'm just an ordinary guy with a professional degree walking a path like everyone else. Tim Faust's and Barbara Brown's book is great even for guys like me. With their emphasis on self-discovery, honesty, spirituality, compassion and kindness, they give the reader new ideas for approaching the difficulties of life.

Daniel Skenderian, Ph. D.
Clinical and Sleep Psychologist

"Soul Retrieval" shows years of experience encouraging, confronting and guiding people through their difficult transitions in life. In this book it is easy for me to see people responding with smiles, deep breaths and new hope. The stories and insights gradually drew me in. There was some-thing to remember on every page and the stories nailed the most valuable ideas into the right spot in the brain.

Tom Linnell, Ed. D
Licensed Psychologist

This book was created by Tim Faust, and is
provided through Harbor North Counseling.

office 715-373-0480
cell 715-209-1045
harbornorth1945@gmail.com.

Soul Retrieval is available as an e-book
or printed softcover book
from Amazon's Kindle Books.
https://www.amazon.com/Kindle-eBooks.

Made in the USA
Columbia, SC
27 April 2020